Ramadan Mubarak!

Adult Coloring Book

This book belongs to

_ _ _ _ _ _ _ _ _ _ _ _ _ _

By Sachin Sachdeva

Copyright © by Sachin Sachdeva

Ramadan is a ninth month of the Islamic calendar,
Muslims greet one another when Ramadan start
by saying, "Ramadan Mubarak" or "Ramadan Kareem"".

Inside this book you'll find hand drawn designs created
to share the love for festival celebrated throughout the world.
The book features 30 unique illustrations of ramadan festival
printed on one side of page. Decorate the blank designs
with your creative doodles.

You can use variety of art materials like watercolors, colored pencils,
markers, crayons, gel pens - they will look stunning on
this high quality, extra thick paper.

The pages designed are handmade and made with pure love :-)

ISBN-13: 978-1098700553

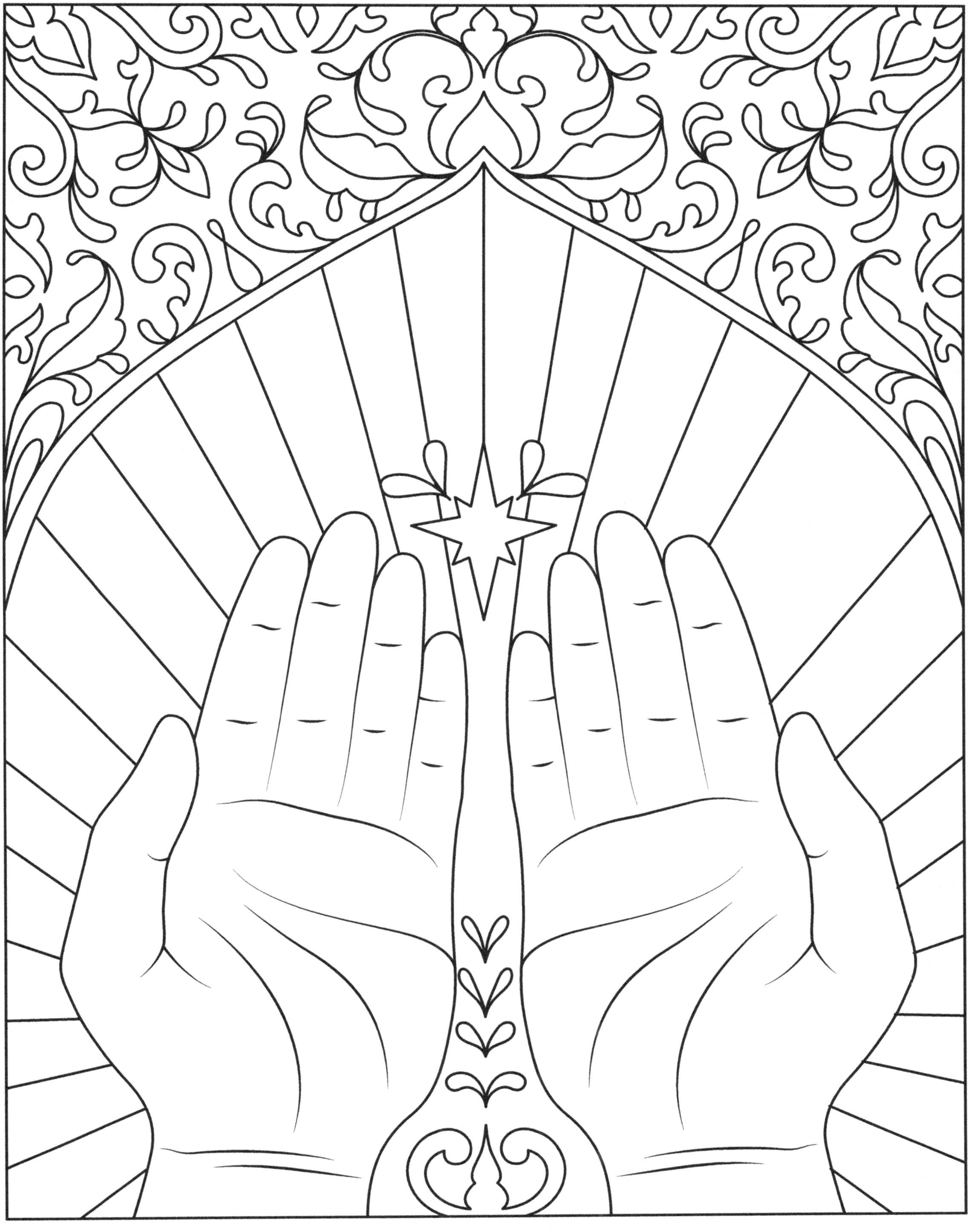

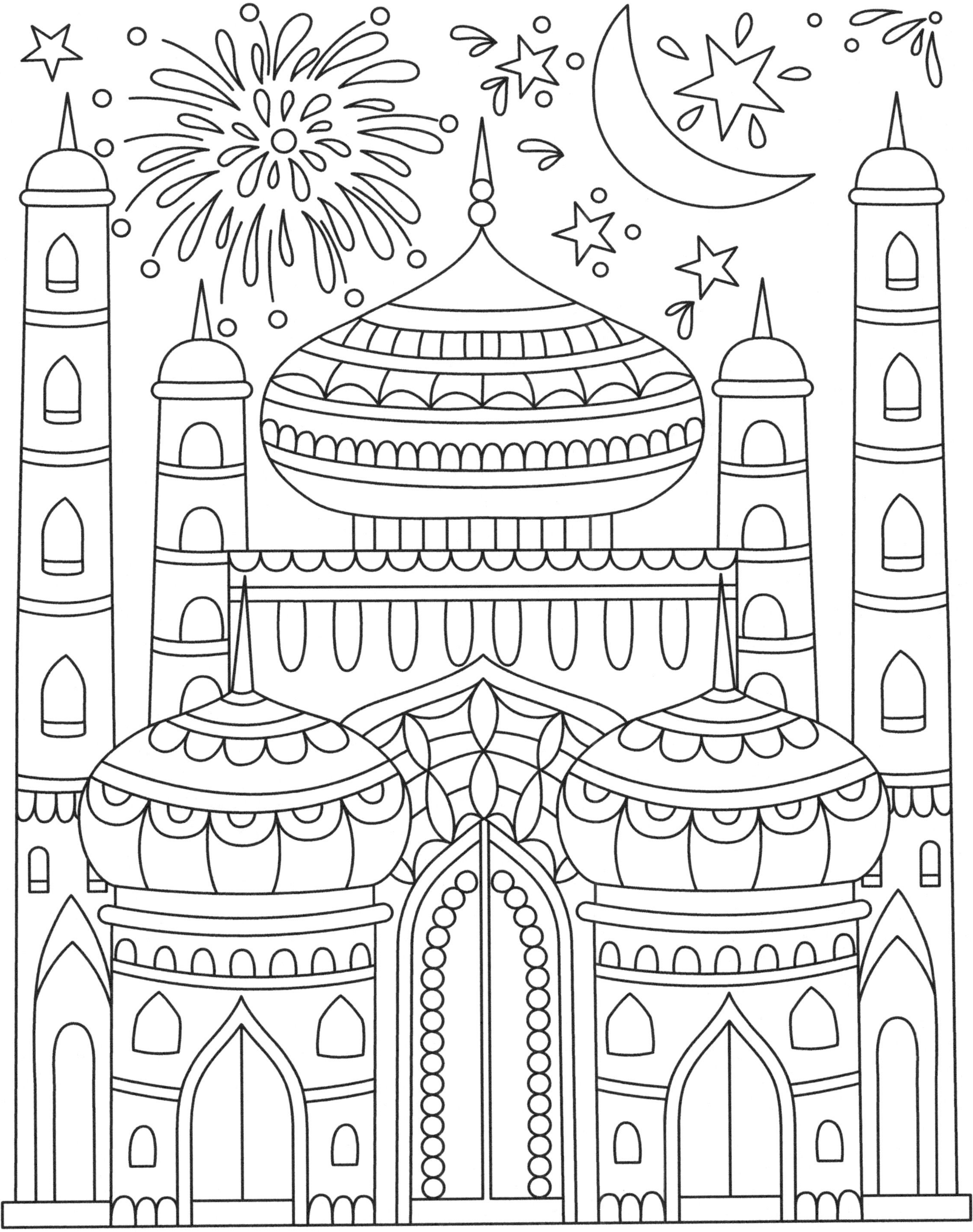

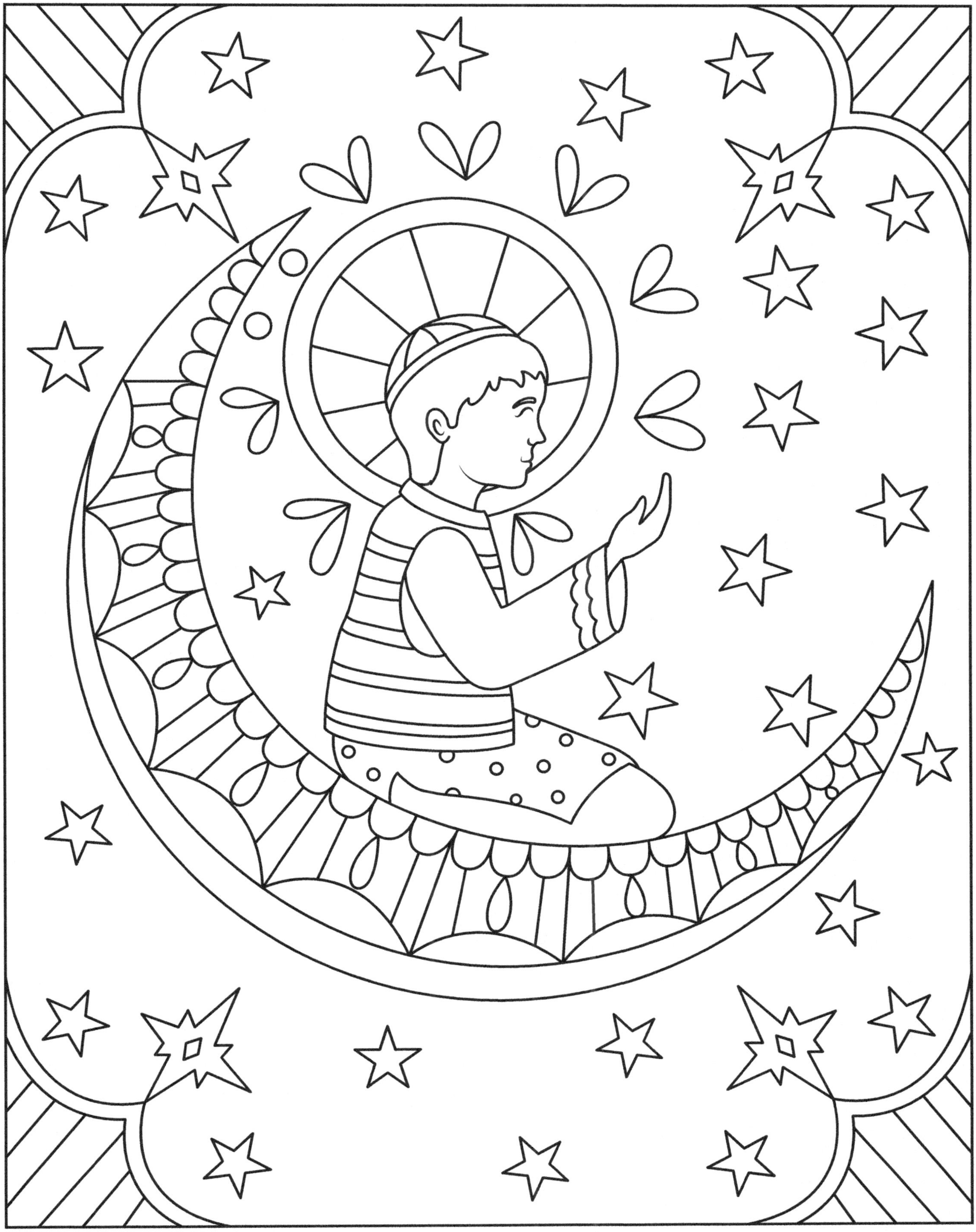

Draw a beautiful design in and around this crescent moon..
Get creative and have fun...

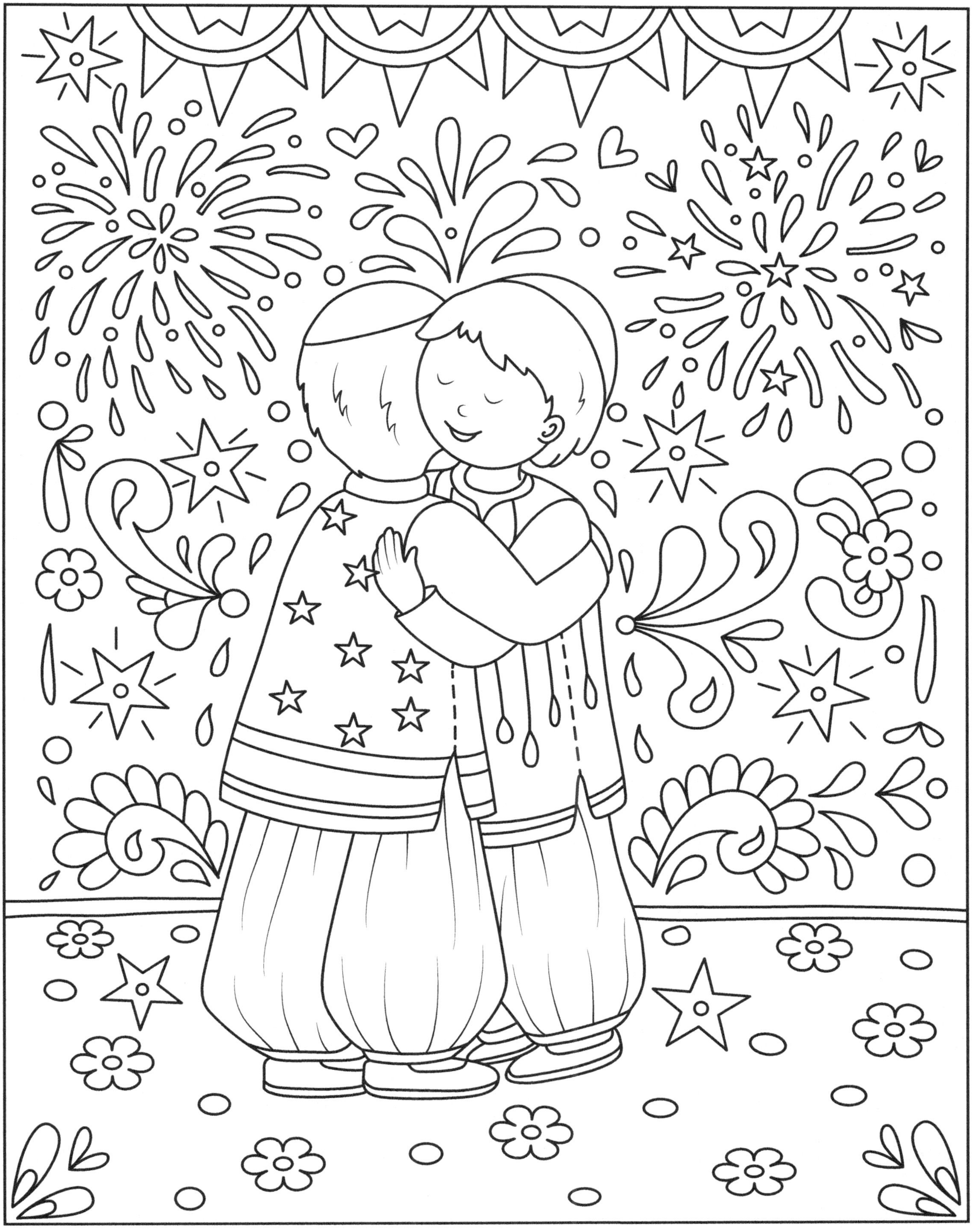

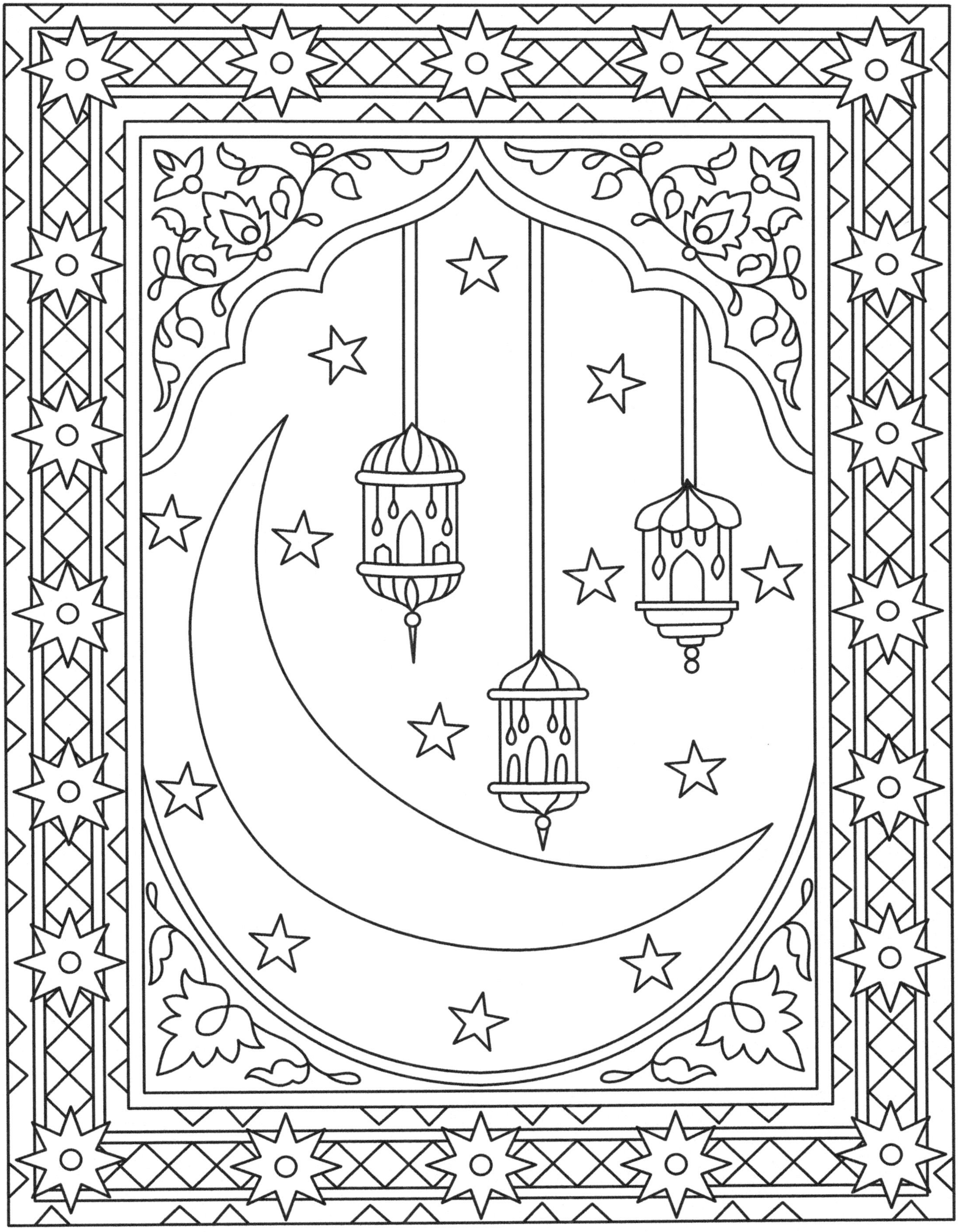

عيد مبارك

Use your imagination to make this artwork
unique & one of a kind...

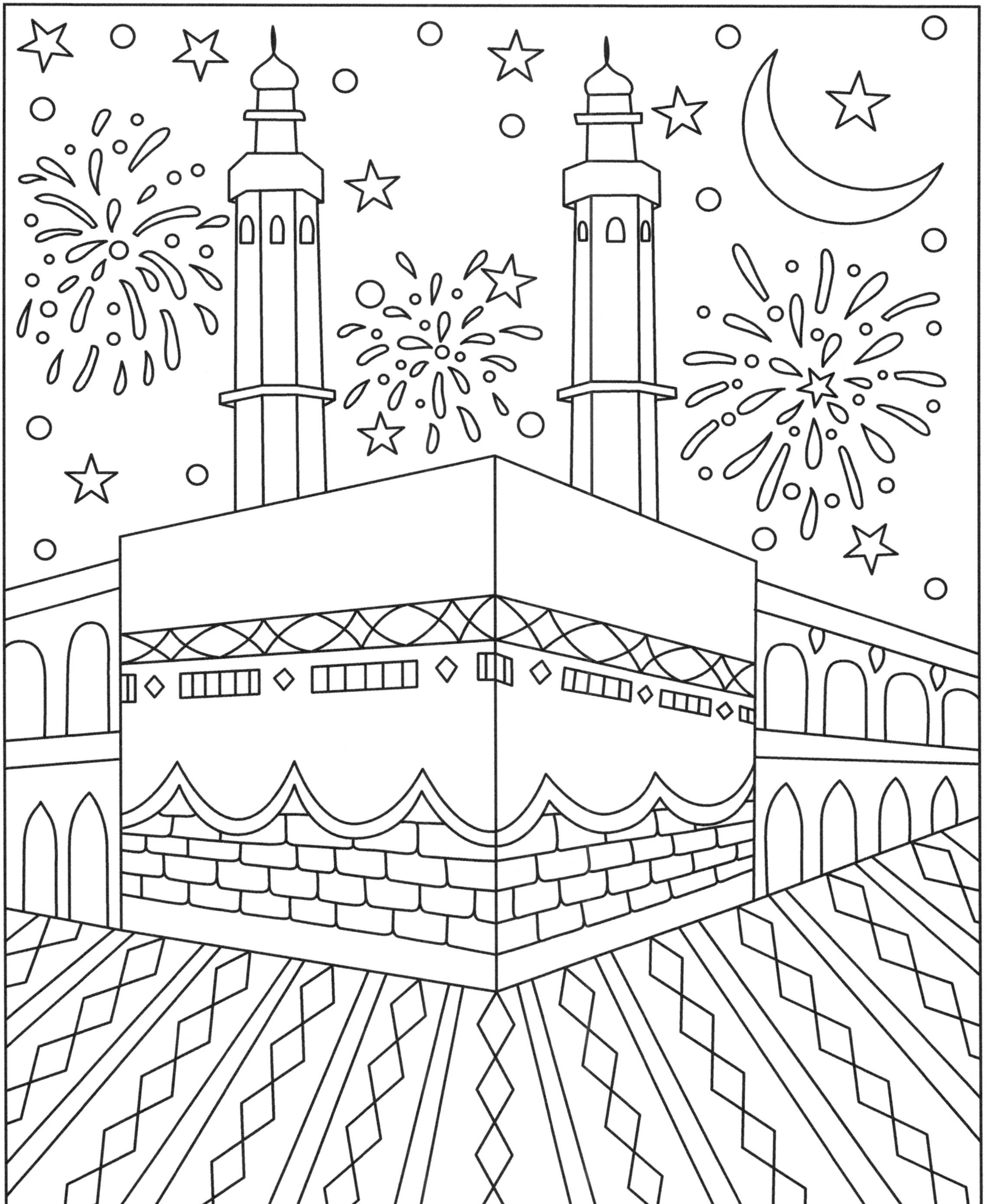

786

Fill this page with your own RAMADAN designs...

Ramadan KAREEM

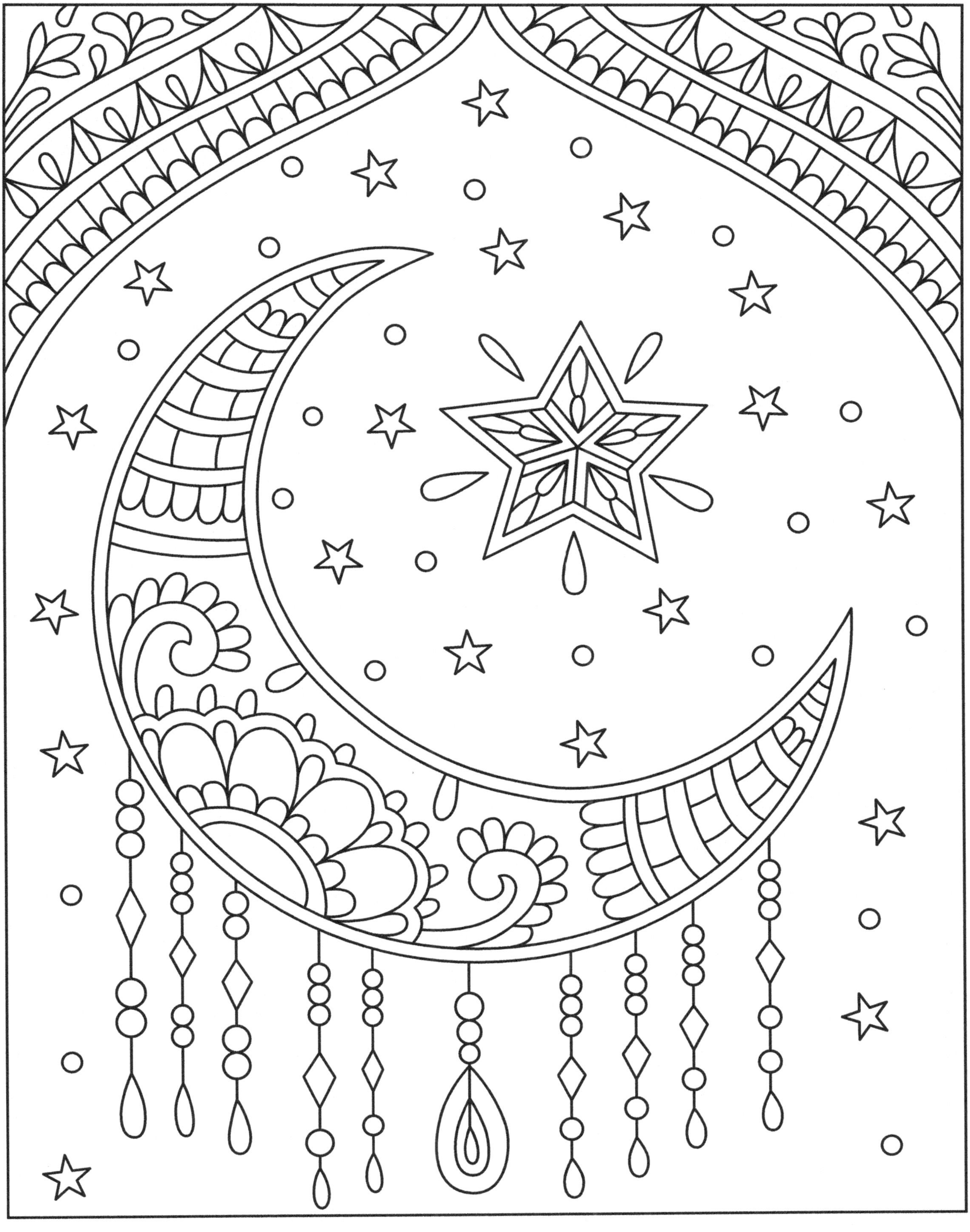

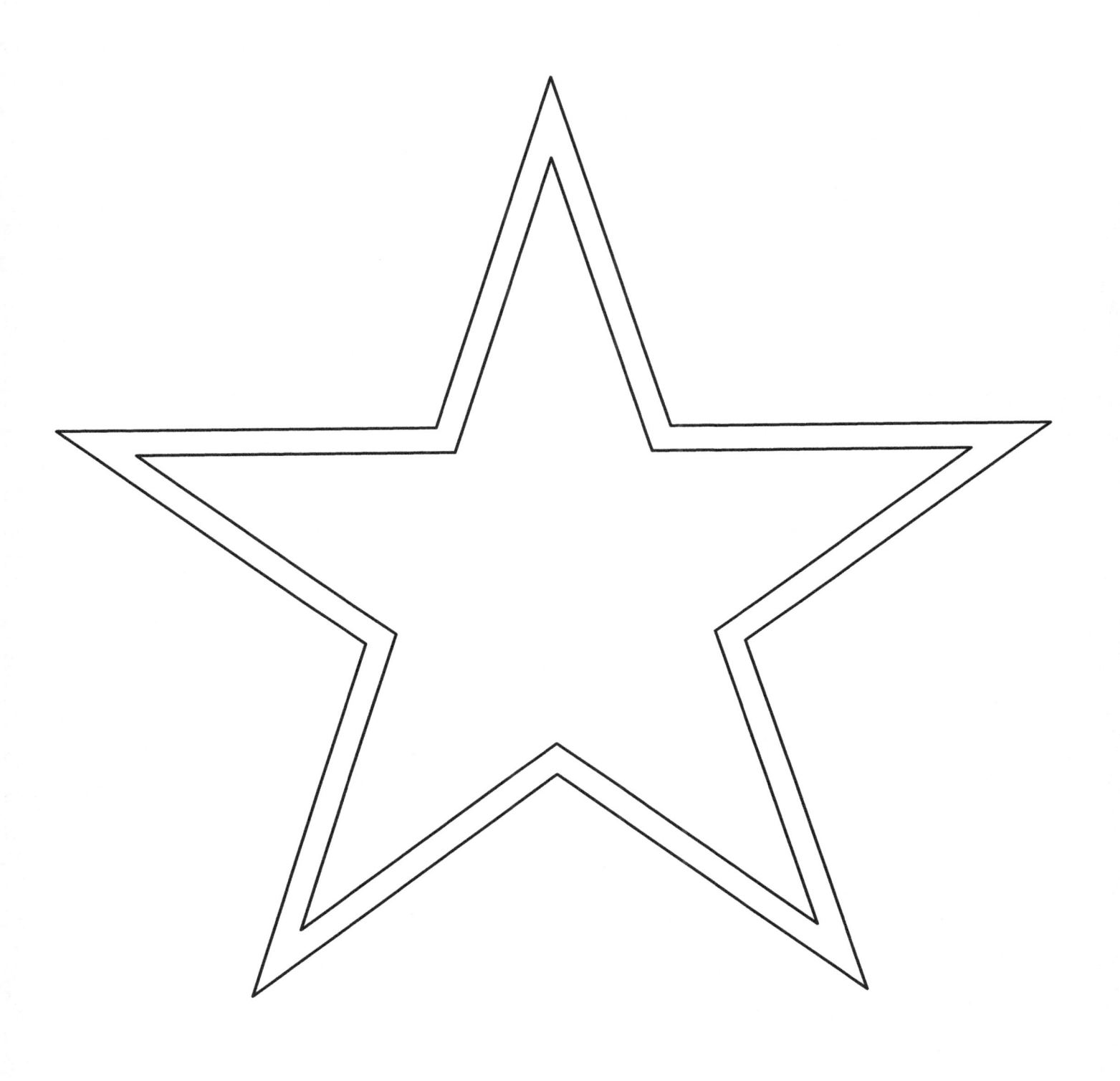

Decorate this star with different patterns and doodeling...

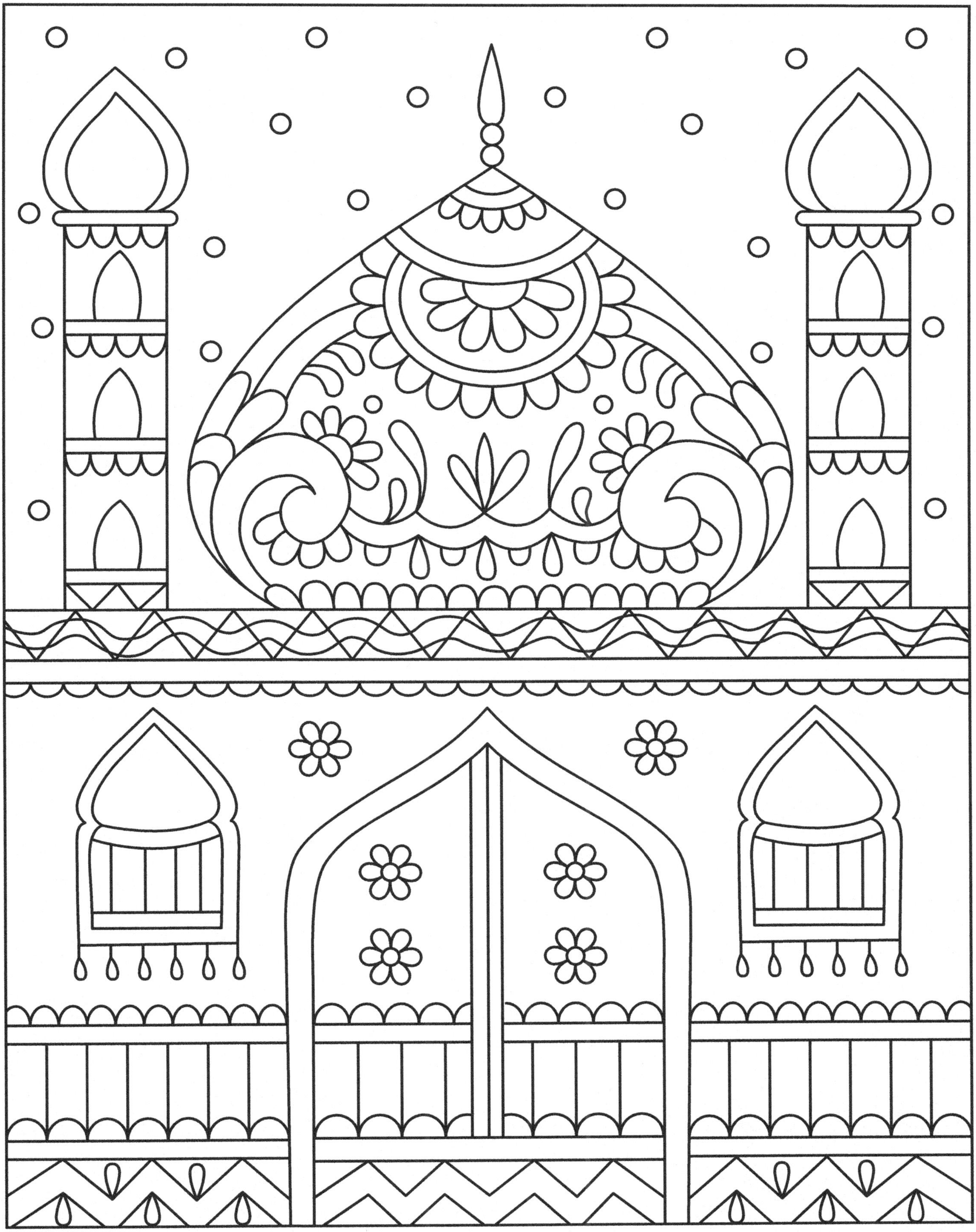

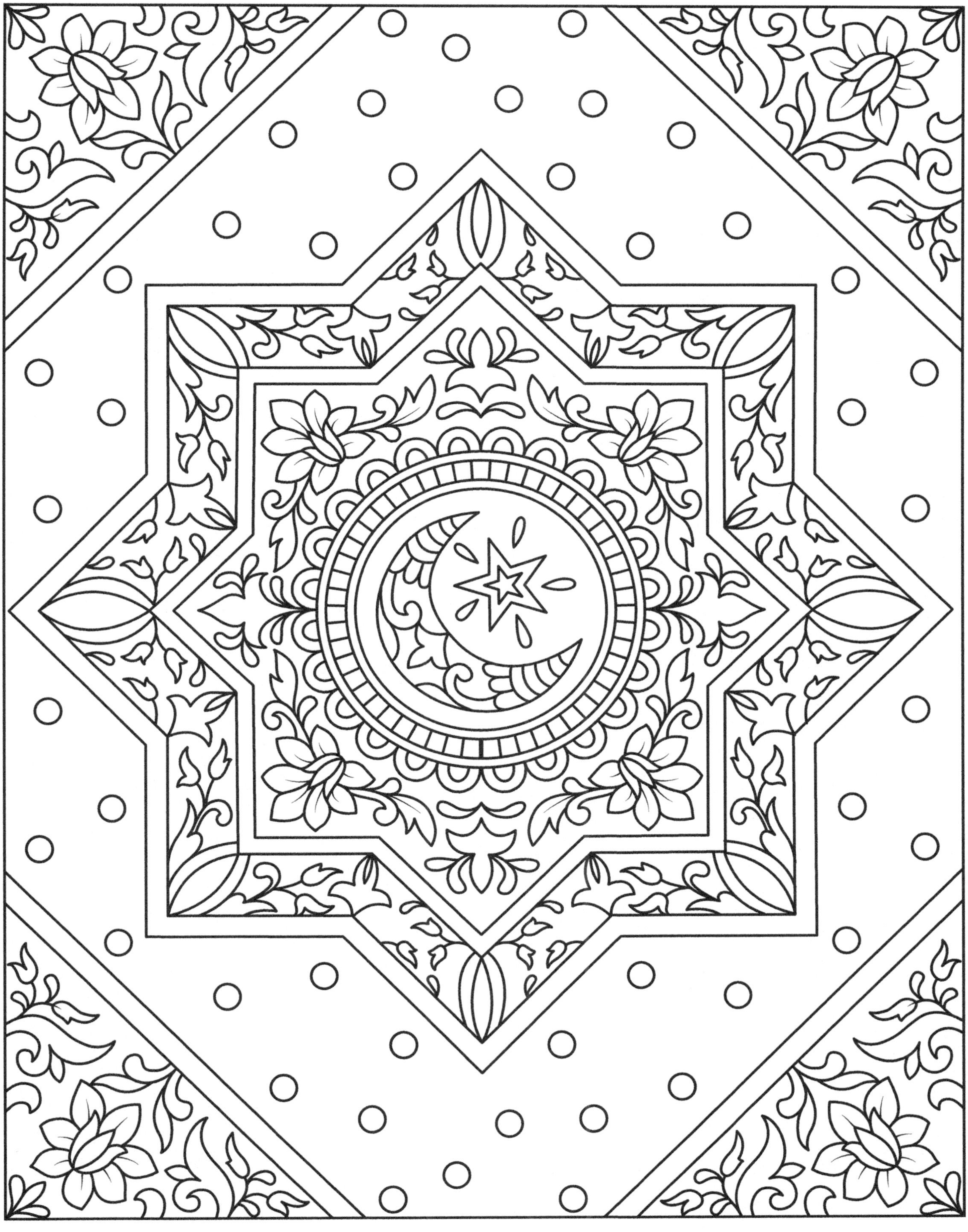

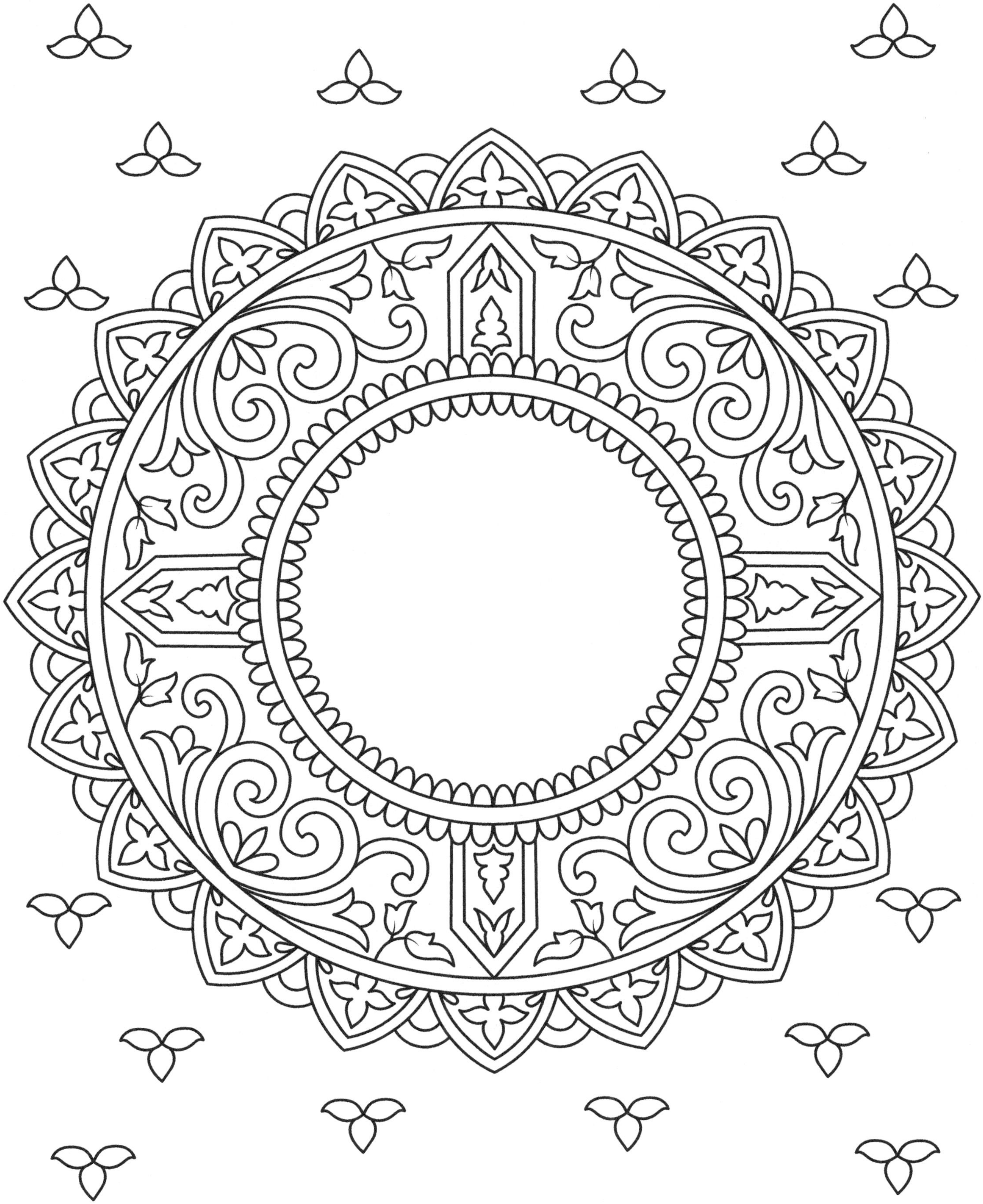

I know you can make this lantern beautiful...

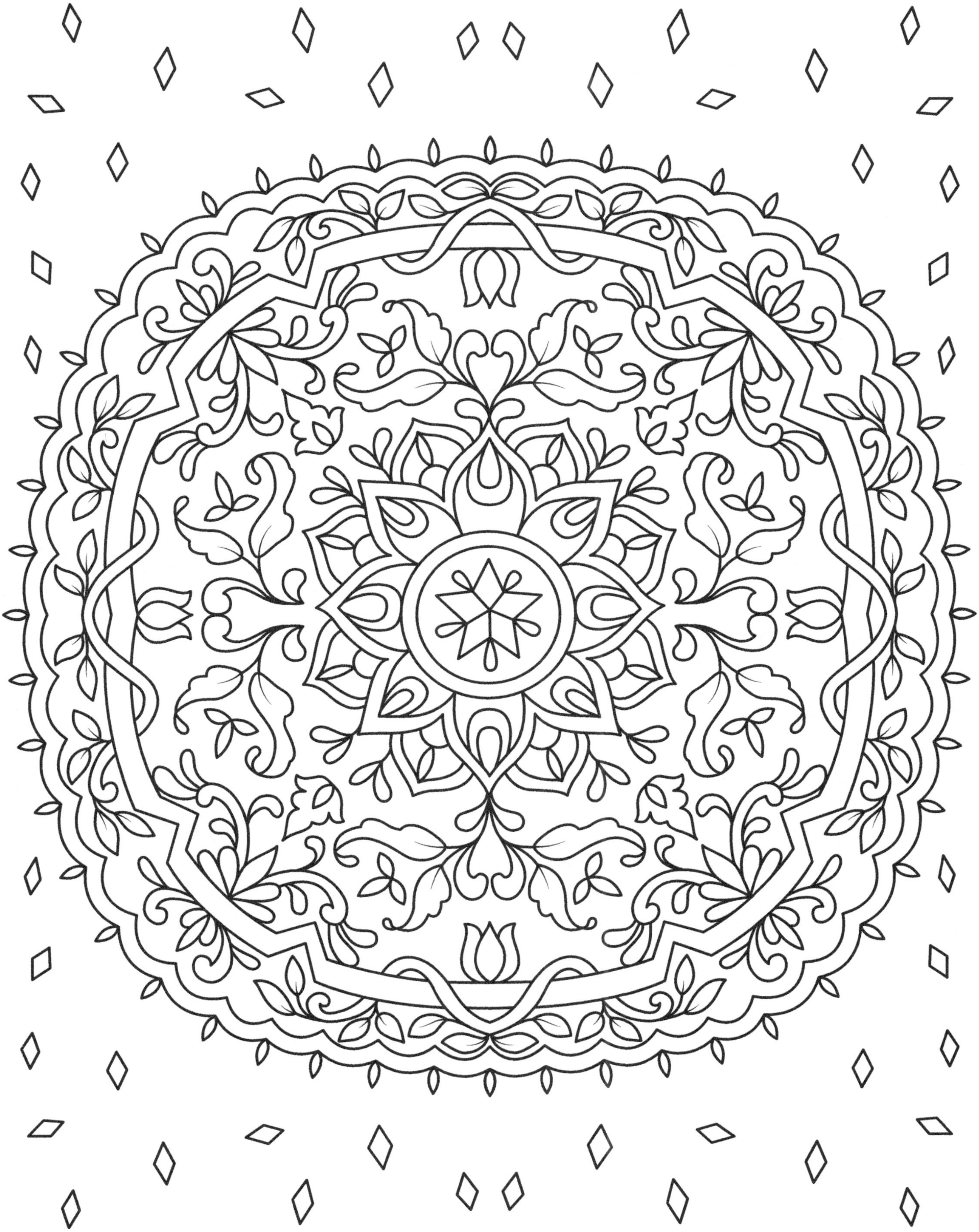

Fill this page with your own Art, Feel Free to draw anything you like…

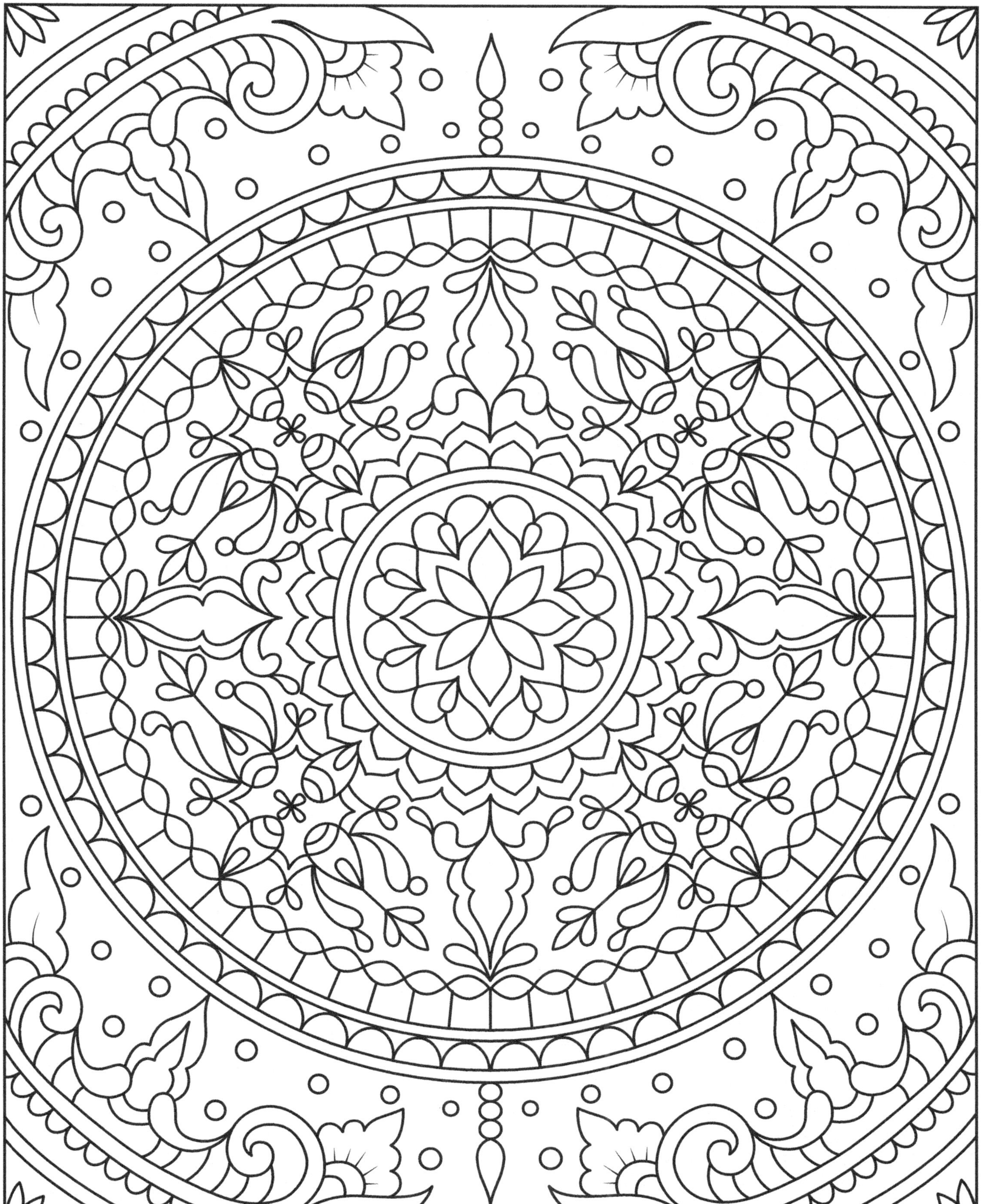

Decorate these lanterns

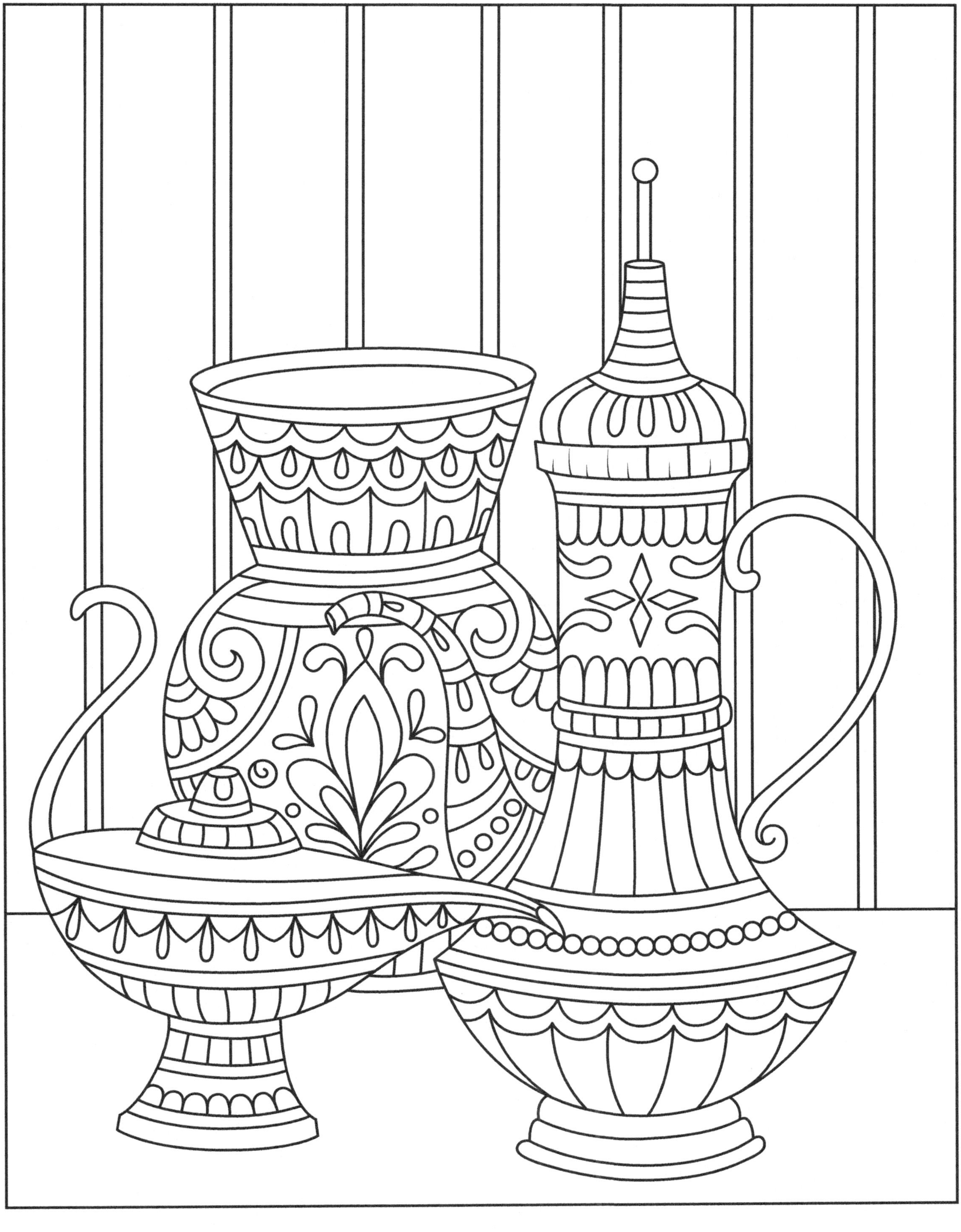

Decorate this design with different patterns and doodeling...

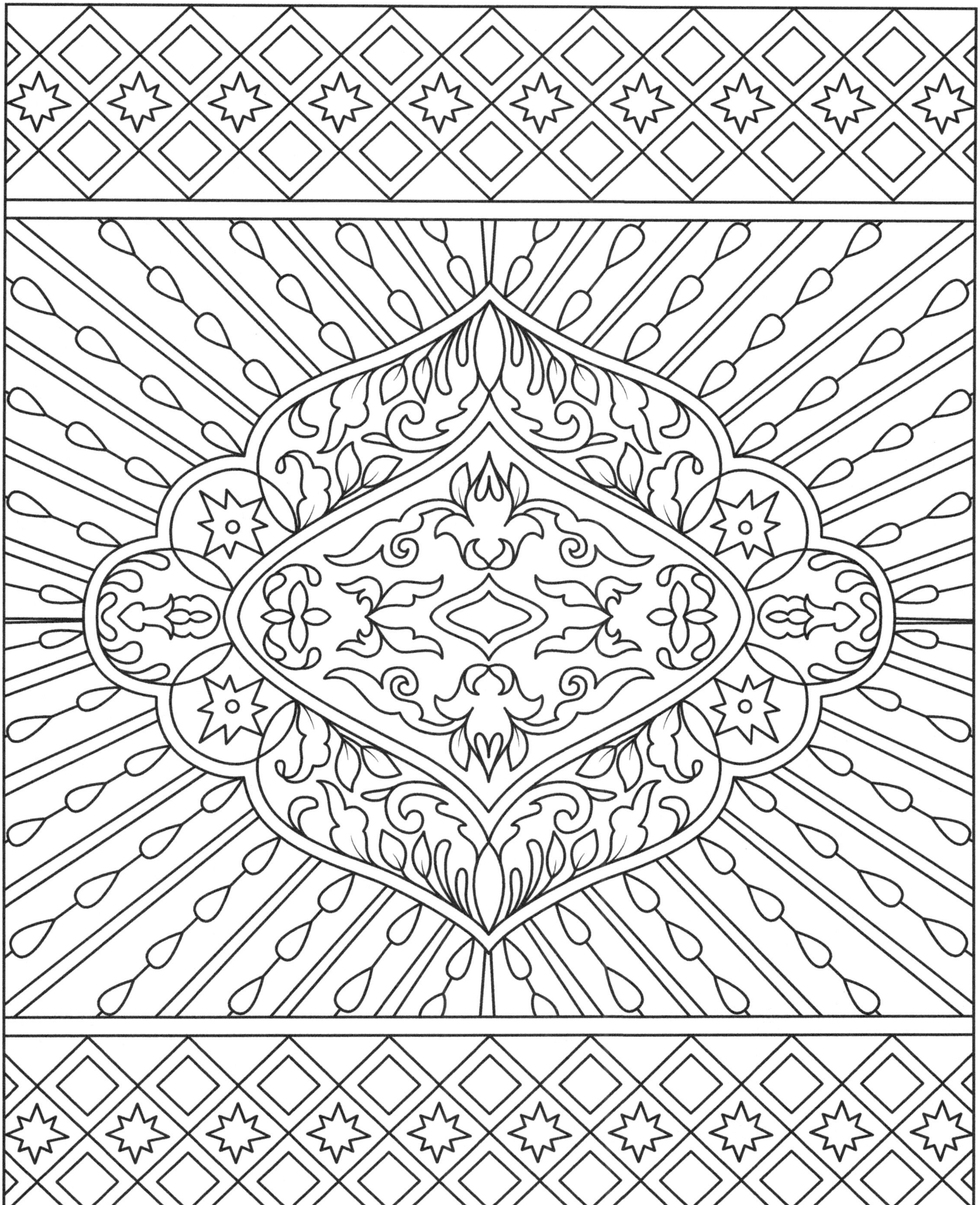

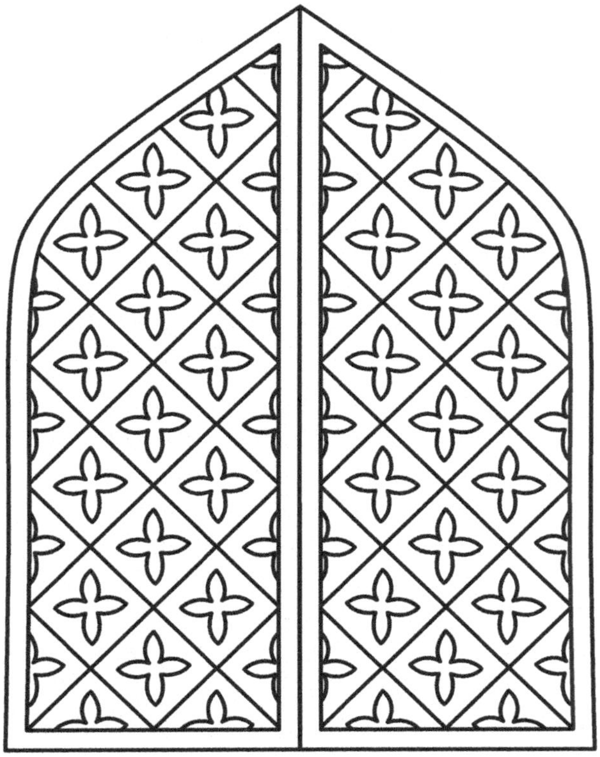
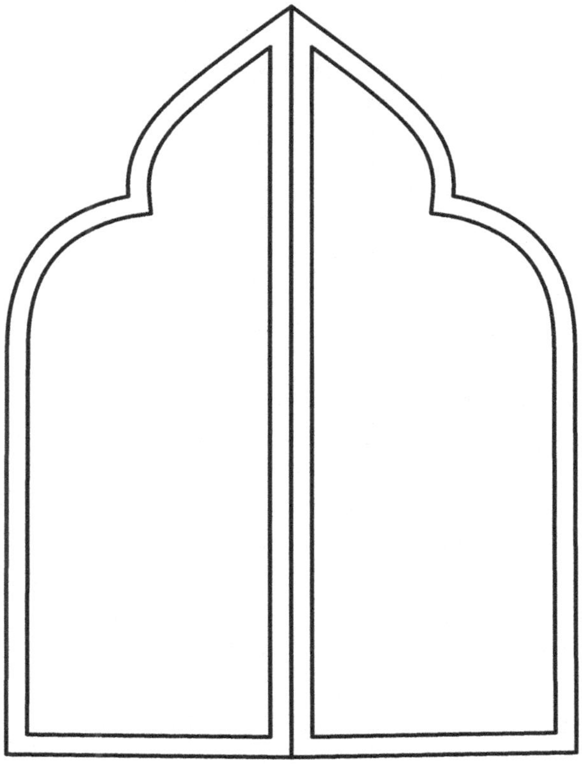
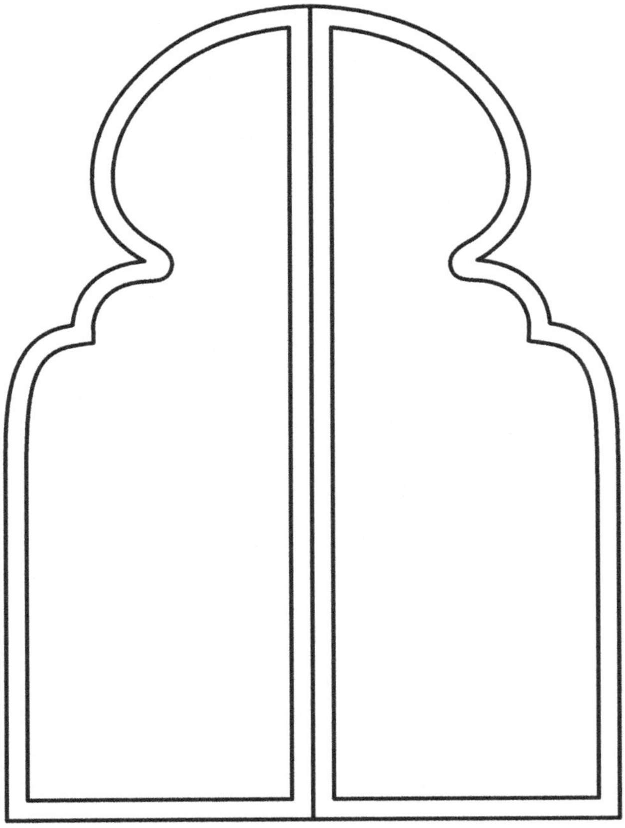
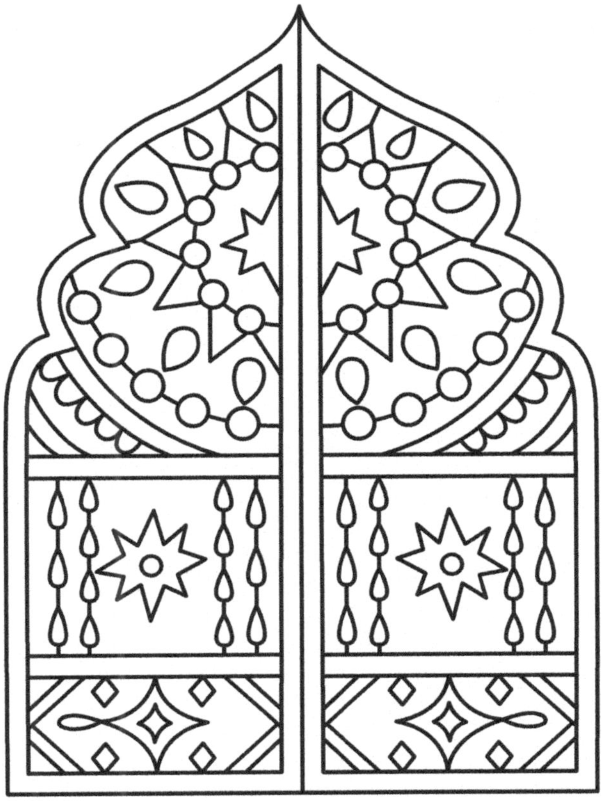

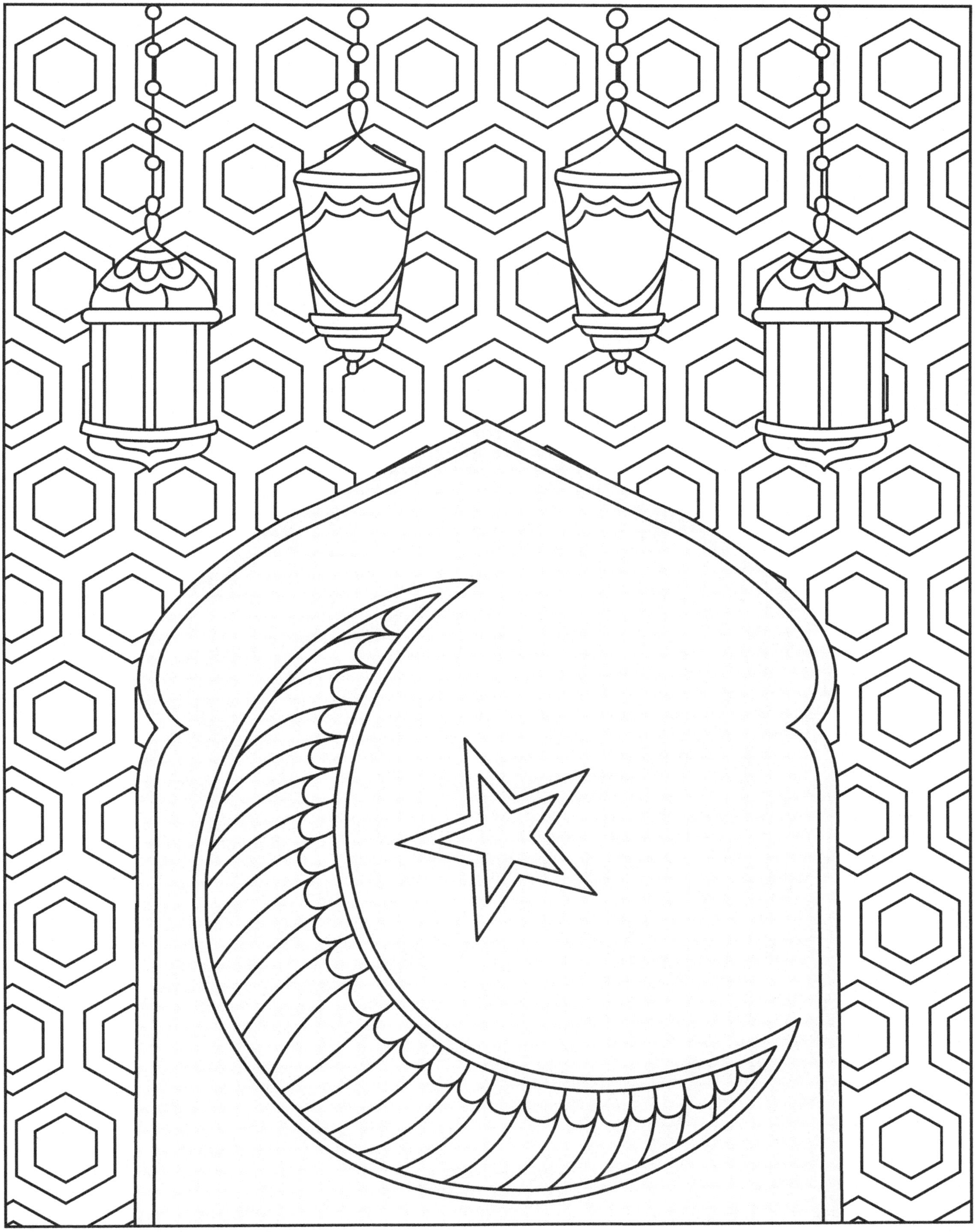

Hope you enjoyed coloring the pages
as much i enjoyed creating them.

Kindly leave your feedback/review on Amazon.
It really helps :)

Thanks,
Sachin Sachdeva
Author & Illustrator

Made in the USA
Monee, IL
28 April 2020